AUTHENTIC HUMANITY

The Human Quest for Reality and Truth

LEONARD SWIDLER, PhD

DEEP-DIALOGUE

CRITICAL-THINKING

EMOTIONALLY-INTELLIGENT

COMPETITIVE-COOPERATION

SPIRITUAL-AIKIDO

Published by iPub Global Connection, LLC

www.iPubCloud.com

1050 W. Nido Avenue, Mesa, AZ 85210

www.iPubCloud.com

info@iPubCloud.com

Paperback 978-1-948575-40-9

About iPubCloud.com

You've opened the right book from the iPub international library. You might be a scholar, an avid reader, a mother or father, a teacher, a 'tween or teen, or one of the rest of us.

Welcome home to iPub Global Connection where knights of old and now digital nomads from all over the world meet safely to share ideas, find resources, and support individuals whose voices wish to be heard to create and protect the world for your great-great-grandchildren.

We are committed to the empowerment of everyone's contributions to a better world. Often, we feel paralyzed by our limiting doubt that alone we have no ability or opportunity to make any real impact.

When that thought comes up, we all need to pick up the eraser in our mind's eye and say "backspace, delete." Individually, together, we can and will influence causing the important changes to ensure a habitable world for future generations….a world embracing global citizenship one by one.

How would *you* begin to define global citizenship? One way might be to remain open enough to learn about other cultures and peoples so that we can connect with all. There are, of course, many ways – through music, art, blogs, podcasts, philosophy, all of which help children model how to be better citizens.

Here you may find what you're looking for, the idea you'd like to expand…a place to be open, to learn, and to trust.

Read on and become a part of the ongoing conversations. Email a note, comment, or share your idea or blog post. Don't keep your views or us a secret. Your voice counts and we care.

This world is in dire need of love, patience, and respect and iPub Publishing is a place where you may find a sentinel in the direction to achieve this transformation. We, along with you, can be a guide towards world peace, improving communication through dialogue, advancing diplomacy among nations to engage with differences. Our international writers, authors, thinkers, and scholars are here to make you think….**Join the renaissance!**

iPub Global Connection, LLC

www.iPubCloud.com

1050 W. Nido Avenue, Mesa, AZ 85210
www.iPubCloud.com
US telephone: 484-775-0008
info@iPubCloud.com

Other iPub Global Connection books may be found at *https://www.ipubcloud.com*

TABLE OF CONTENTS

i

Introduction

You are beginning a journey of a uniquely human quest for deep-truth, authentic reality, which is at the heart of Leonard Swidler's exploration of our humanness in *Authentic Humanity*. Travelers and thinkers interested in his interpretation of both the corporal and the spiritual will find this book not just informative, but also probing, provocative. He continually asks: Is something real because it in fact is real, or because we interpret it as real? Then: What is truth? Is our understanding fact-based, logical—is it, perhaps, even more? Can we agree on certain truths, or is everything subject to individual interpretation?

As Swidler notes: *"All* knowledge is interpreted knowledge." We "know" what we know as we find meaning and significance based on both our individual experience and our collective awareness, our individual understanding and our shared agreement on what something means, on what something truly is and is not. This shared conclusion is especially relevant today when our quest for meaning, truth, and purpose seems ever more distant, and yet takes center stage in many things we do. Is ongoing human conflict the result of misinterpretation, or poor dialogue, communication about these "findings?"

Our knowledge is potentially unlimited in that we clearly don't know everything. Yet, individual and collective conclusions about reality, and our dialogue about it can be transformative individually and collectively. We compare notes with each other, and through this interaction we come to a mutual understanding of "the truth"—through shared dialogue.

What is known is limited by our "receptors," our interpretation of what we perceive. Therefore, we wrestle continually with our interpretation/s. Is what we see or know all that there is? Or is there much more that we are not tuned into, cannot see, or lack the ability to fully understand?

Dr. Swidler presents a classic interpretation of human perception through his methodical and historically-based examination of what is "known" to be true, and the many ways we engage in dialogue to share our findings of that truth, our personal grasp of it—our take on what we see, hear and feel. It is not just about a collective awareness of reality or the truth but, importantly, about how we communicate to, or dialogue with each other about those findings. Swidler's provocative and accessible book follows in the tradition of his acclaimed biblical and historical research, but adds a modern twist of acknowledging the place of technology in the modern world.

Authentic Humanity illustrates the multiple levels of human dialogue from the foundation of "understanding" the cosmos, through critical thinking, deliberative analysis, to intuitive thinking, imagination, to human spiritual awareness. It offers an overview of what

Swidler calls mens sana incorpore sano (a healthy mind in a healthy body).

It synthesizes what it means to be authentically human.

This book provides a framework of the thinking process, of our uniquely human tendency to analyze everything. This book will:

· Help explore physical-spiritual, individual-communal, human-cosmos reality, and their interpretation(s)

· Highlight why dialogue among all of us about perception-expression can provide us tested-broadened-deepened perspectives on our human existence

· Provide an enhanced understanding of the human thinking process

· Help us comprehend our need to explore, explain, and dialogue about our perceptions

· Help reveal what constitutes *Authentic Humanity*.

...

1. "All Knowledge Is Interpreted Knowledge"

To begin, we humans, as a group, have in the last two centuries increasingly learned that "*Nobody knows Everything about Anything!*" We now know that *all knowledge is interpreted knowledge*. There is no "truth" out there. There is "reality" out there, but "truth" resides in our knowing capacities: senses, sensitivities, and intellect. Normally we use the words "truth" and "true" to refer to our *statements* about something. We would say that my statement, "The door is closed," is true if the statement accurately described reality – in this case, that the door is in fact closed. At the same time, naturally we can say many other "true" things about the door; for example, that it is so tall, so wide, is a particular color, made of wood, and on and on indefinitely. Our potential knowledge of that door is endless, except that it is limited by our "receptors." If I know little, for example, about chemistry, my knowing about the chemical makeup of the door is thereby limited.

If this is true about a simple physical object, how much more is it true about more complicated, abstract matters, such as are claimed in understandings of literature, political affairs, history – and especially that most comprehensive of all "disciplines," religion ("*An explanation of the **total** meaning of life, and how to live accordingly*" – if based on some notion of the transcendent, however understood, then called "religion," if not, then called, perhaps, "ideology")? The all-encompassing meaning of claims in the Bible, Qur'an, or Vedas will necessarily be limited by my knowing capacities. If I am a believing Muslim, for example, the Qur'an will not impact my life until it has gotten into my knowing capacities, my senses, sensitivities, and intellect. But, like liquid Jell-O being poured into its container, it – in this case, the meanings of the Qur'an – takes the shape of the container. The "truth" of the Qur'an will take the shape of my senses, sensitivities, and intellect. Analogously this is the case with all religious believers (or for whatever passes in a person's life as religion, or ideology). So, if I am the kind of Catholic who says, "whatever the pope says is true," then *I* have decided that "truth" will take the shape of "whatever the pope says," or analogously, if *I* as a Muslim say "whatever the Sheikh says the Qur'an says, *I* accept" or on the other hand, *I* say that *I* will decide for myself what is the ultimate meaning of life, or, or, or.... There is no escape from the fact that *I* am intimately involved in *all* knowledge, that "All knowledge is interpreted knowledge."

Am I then trapped in a destructive solipsism (Latin: *solus*, "alone"; *ipsus*, "myself"), a "Leonard Swidler" bubble? No, for we humans can communicate with other "knowers," who also necessarily perceive the world from their own vantage points, as I do from mine. That gives us the possibility of learning about other facets of reality— seen from, e.g., Mary Murphy's perspective, or from Mutombo Nkulu's perspective, so that I can compare, analyze their knowledge and aim at gaining an ever fuller – but never complete and never totally "objective" grasp of reality. In a word, the only way we can endlessly escape our "Myself Alone" bubble is by *Dialogue*. I need to come to know about reality as perceived and understood by, e.g., a Chinese Buddhist woman, who clearly will perceive and understand facets of reality that I as an American Catholic man cannot perceive and understand from my experience of reality, and vice versa. In short, we both need to be in Dialogue with each other, and everyone else – endlessly! This is a far deeper, life-transforming understanding of Dialogue of which I speak than the often now rather superficial common understanding. Hence, I increasingly use the expanded term *Deep Dialogue* to get at this more profound, substantial, life-shaping meaning.

2. **Dialogue is the Very Foundation of the Cosmos**

Dialogue – understood at its broadest as the mutually beneficial interaction of differing components – is at the very heart of the Universe of which we humans are the highest expression. On the *macro* level – from the basic interaction of matter *and* energy (in Einstein's unforgettable formula, $E=MC^2$; *E*nergy equals *M*ass times the square of the *Speed of Light [C]*), to the *micro* level, the creative interaction of protons *and* electrons in every atom, to the vital symbiosis of body *and* spirit in every human, through the creative Dialogue between woman *and* man, to the dynamic relationship between individual *and* society. Thus, the very essence of our humanity is dialogical, and a fulfilled human life is the highest expression of the "*Cosmic Dance of Dialogue*."

In the early millennia of the history of humanity, as we spread outward from our starting point in central Africa 200,000 years ago, the forces of *di*vergence were dominant. However, because we live on a globe, in our frenetic *di*vergence we eventually began to encounter each other more and more frequently. Now, the forces of stunning *con*vergence are becoming increasingly dominant.

In the past, during the Age of *Di*vergence, we could live in isolation from each other; we could ignore each other. Now, in the Age of *Con*vergence, we are forced to live in one world. We increasingly live in a Global Village. We cannot ignore the Other, the Different. Too often in the past we have tried to make over the Other into a likeness of ourselves, often by violence, but this is the very opposite of Dialogue. This egocentric arrogance is in fundamental opposition to the "*Cosmic Dance of Dialogue.*" It is not creative; it is destructive. Hence, we humans today have a stark choice: *Dialogue, or Death!*[1]

---

[1] See Leonard Swidler, with John Cobb, Monika Hellwig, and Paul Knitter, *Death or Dialogue: From the Age of Monologue to the Age of Dialogue* (Philadelphia: Trinity Press International, 1990).

3. Dialogues of the Head, Hands, Heart in Holistic Harmony of the Holy Human

For us humans there are three main dimensions to Dialogue, corresponding to the structure of our humanness: Dialogue of the H*ead*, H*ands*, H*eart*, in H*olistic* H*armony* of the H*oly* H*uman*.

a. Dialogue of the Head: The Cognitive/Intellectual: Seeking the True

In the Dialogue of the *Head,* we reach out to those who think differently from us to understand how they see the world and why they act as they do. The world is too complex for anyone to grasp alone; increasingly, we can understand reality only with the help of the other, in Dialogue. This is important, because how we *understand* the world determines how we *act* in the world.

b. Dialogue of the Hands – The Illative or Ethical: Seeking the Good

In the Dialogue of the *Hands,* we join with others to work to make the world a better place in which we all must live together. Since we can no longer live separately in this "one world," we must work jointly to make it not just a house but a *home* for all of us to live in. In other words, we join hands with the other to "heal the world" – *Tikkun olam*, in the Jewish tradition. The world within us and

<11>11</11>

around us is always in need of healing, and our deepest wounds can be healed only together with the Other, only in Dialogue.

c. Dialogue of the Heart – to The Affective or Aesthetic: Seeking the Beautiful, the Spiritual

In the Dialogue of the *Heart* we open ourselves to receive the beauty of the Other. Because we humans are body and spirit – or, rather, body-spirit – to we give bodily spiritual expression in all the arts with our multifarious responses to life: Joy, sorrow, gratitude, anger, and, most of all, love. We try to express our inner feelings, which grasp reality in far deeper and higher ways than we are able to put into rational concepts and words; hence, we create poetry, music, dance, painting, architecture – the expressions of the heart. All the world delights in beauty, and so it is here that we find the easiest encounter with the Other, the simplest door to Dialogue. Here, too, is where the depth, spiritual, mystical dimension of the human spirit is given full rein. As 17th-century mathematician/philosopher Blaise Pascal said, *Le cœur a ses raisons que la raison ne connaît point.* "The heart has its reasons, which reason knows not."

d. Dialogue of Wholeness—Holiness:[2] Seeking the One

We humans cannot live a divided life. If we are to survive, let alone flourish, we must "get it all together." We must not only dance the Dialogues of the Head, Hands, and Heart but also bring our various parts together in Harmony (a fourth "H") to live a Holistic (a fifth "H"), life, which is what religions mean that we should be Holy (from the Greek *holos*, "whole"). Hence, we are authentically Human (a seventh "H") only when our manifold elements are in Dialogue within each other, and we are in Dialogue with the others around us. We must dance together the "*Cosmic Dance of Dialogue*" of the Head, Hands, and Heart, Holistically, in Harmony[3] within the Holy Human.

---

[2] The popular notion of "Holy" as attributed to someone who spends huge amounts of time in praying, fasting, and the like, somehow separated from ordinary human life, is *exactly wrong*. To be holy literally means to be "whole," "healthy." The English language is made up mostly from Greek or Latin and German terms. On the Latin side we have key terms like "salvation," and "saved," which stem from *salus*, "health"; hence, cognates like "salutary," "salubrious," and "salute." On the Germanic side we have the key term *Heil*, "health," from which we have English cognates such as "health," "hale," and "whole." The latter, "whole," can be traced back even further to the Greek *holos*, "whole." German Christians, for example, say that Jesus is their *Heiland*, "Savior," the one who makes us spiritually "healthy," hence, "holy," that is, "whole."

[3] Those who know Western medieval philosophy will recognize that these are the "Metaphysicals," the four aspects of Being Itself, perceived from different perspectives: the One, the True, the Good, the Beautiful.

4. Deep Dialogue Entails Critical Thinking

a. Meaning of Terms

If we reflect at all about the term *Dialogue,* it will be clear that it is about *thinking.*[4] The Greek prefix *dia* has a variety of meanings, including: across, among, together. The Greek word *logos* is familiar to all speakers of Western languages in its many cognates, starting with *logic* – the science of *thinking* clearly. Further, all the words ending in "logy," like geology, psychology, anthropology mean the systematic *thinking* about the *geos* (earth), *psyche* (spirit), *anthropos* (human). Thus, *dia-logos* means *thinking*across or *thinking*together, making it clear that at the heart of *dia-logos*, Dialogue, is *thinking*, and not just any thinking, but *systematic* thinking, *logical* thinking, that is: *Critical Thinking*.

Hence, if Dialogue is at the foundation of the whole Cosmos, with the human as its conscious pinnacle, the lead Dancer of the "Cosmic Dance of Dialogue," it is also true that *logos*, thinking, is at the center of Dialogue, at the center of the Cosmos (Greek: *cosmos* = "order"; *chaos* = "confusion"; we humans are constantly learning

---

[4] *Think* comes from the Germanic side of the English (Anglo-Saxon) language: *denken* is "to think," "to cogitate" (Latin: *cogitare* = "to think").

15

progressively more about the *logos*, the "order," the *cosmos* – which persists even in the midst of, seemingly to us at times, *chaos*, "confusion" – that permeates all reality). If we are seriously to engage in Dialogue, in Deep-Dialogue, we necessarily must also engage in *logos*, logic, *denken*, thinking: *Critical Thinking*.

The first thing to recognize about the term *Critical Thinking* is that it does not mean negatively "criticizing" someone or something. Rather, the term "critical" comes from the Greek *krinein*, "to make a judgment, a decision." However, we can make a judgment, a decision, thoughtfully (with systematic *denken*, *logos*, "logic") only if we have the data in front of us so that we can first *analyze* it (Greek: *ana*, "up," *lysis,* "break"), i.e., to break up the ideas, the information, into their component parts to see how they fit together, and then move to *synthesis* (Greek: *syn* "together," *thesis,* "to put"), that is, after seeing how the component parts fit together. We explore the relations of the parts to other things, or at times to put the parts together in new ways.

b. The Three "W" Questions: What? Whence? Whither?

If *analysis* and *synthesis* are the fundamental ways we humans think, in order to think critically, to make a judgment, a decision, on the basis of gathered data and systematic, analytic-synthetic thought, we must first address three basic "*W*" questions: *What, Whence, Whither?*

What? means that we need to develop the *habit* of striving to understand as *precisely* as possible what it is we are talking about. This principle is so obvious that it tends, as so often in life, to be violated in proportion to its simplicity. Oftentimes, it helps to ask what the etymological roots of the term in question are (as I have been doing here) to help get a clear grasp of what we are talking about. Example: *to believe* means having *faith* in someone or something; "Faith" comes from the Latin *fides*, "having trust." Hence, believing something, having faith in something, means affirming that something is true, not because we have proof of it, but because we *trust* the source of that information—Mom, pastor, Qur'an, Bible….

We also need to make sure that I and my interlocutors have *precisely the same understanding* of the idea or term being discussed; otherwise, we will simply be talking past each other. It is also especially vital that we keep precisely the same meaning of the term when we move from one statement to another. If we don't, we will end up with a – false! – *four-term syllogism*. A typical syllogism runs like this:

A is E

E is C

Therefore,

A is C

We need to be certain that the meaning of the connecting term, "E," has precisely the same meaning in the second premise as in the first. If, however, deliberately or inadvertently, we change the meaning, however slightly, of the connecting term – E to È – while keeping the same sound, we will have a *four-term syllogism*:

A is E

È is C

Therefore,

...?

Therefore, nothing (!) simply because we have four terms: A, E, È, and C. Hence, it is vital to know precisely *What* we are talking about.

In thinking, alone or with others, out loud or in writing, we start with an idea or term – and, as just noted, in answering the first question of *What?* we need to be clear about its precise meaning. Secondly, we need to ask ourselves, *Whence?* Where does the basis for affirming this idea come from? Are we beginning by simply defining something to be the case? Is this idea an unexamined presupposition? Do we have factual evidence for it? Is it a valid, logical deduction from solidly proven data? Is it based on a trustworthy source? etc., etc. Any truthful results of thinking, alone, or with others, will depend on the validity of the answer to this question: *Whence* the evidence for what we are talking about? Does the information come from an eyewitness, a third-hand or fifth-hand one, or someone that is biased for or against the claim, and the like.

If we have been careful in understanding precisely *What* we are talking about and carefully tested the basis – the *Whence* – for our affirming the idea in question, then we need to ask ourselves where – *Whither?* – this idea leads to. What are its implications, for if the idea is true, then we want to base our subsequent actions on it. In other words, ideas have consequences! Example: If the Golden Rule is judged to be a valid ethical principle, then I need to respect others, tell the truth to others, help others.... because I would want them to treat me the same way.

Secondly, it is important to follow these implications to their conclusion to learn whether or not they lead to a *reductio ad absurdum* ("reduction to absurdity"). If that turns out to be the case, then we will need to reinvestigate our databases and whole line of reasoning from the beginning in order to find the flaw of fact or logic. Example: Some Christian theologians (e.g., Augustine, Luther, and Calvin) argued that nothing can happen except that God *causes* it to happen, including *causing* humans to commit sins which will condemn them to hell for all eternity – the doctrine of "predestination." But, for followers of Jesus who depicted God as His loving Father who reaches out to all humans to lead them to Himself, this is a clear contradiction, a *reductio ad absurdum* – a loving God deliberately creating humans, not to lead them to God, but to hell! This line of critical thinking led many Augustinians, Lutherans, and Calvinists to reject the doctrine of predestination.

c. Unconscious Presuppositions

A further fundamental move we must strive to make in order to engage in Critical Thinking concerns our *Un*conscious *Pre*suppositions. To be conscious of something is, naturally, to be aware of it. Obviously, *un*-conscious means to *not* be aware of something. Also, clearly *pre* (Latin) means "beforehand," and *sup-position* (Latin: *sub-positio* = under-position) means something *under-lying*. Hence, a *pre*supposition is an idea that ahead of time *underlies* another idea or set of ideas. When speaking of an *un*conscious *pre*supposition, it is one that we already have in our mind, but of which we are *un*aware; it is *un*conscious. For example: previously, and unfortunately still today, many men and women considered women incapable of clear, rational thought. This was a *pre*supposition, a prior underlying assumption, that prevented women from attending the university. For the most part, it was *un*conscious, that is, most did not think about it, they just assumed it without being aware that they were doing so.

So long as a *pre*supposition remains uninvestigated, we cannot know whether we are acting on the basis of reality or mirage. We cannot truthfully tell ourselves that we are acting thus in a rational manner. The situation is even vastly more devastating when the *pre*supposition is *un*conscious. Then, we are controlled totally by an idea that might be partially, or even totally, unwarranted – and we can do absolutely nothing about it (!) for we are powerless to analyze an idea, and change the consequent action, if we do not even know of the existence of the idea, which is the motor that drives our mind and behavior.

We all have endless numbers of *un*conscious *pre*suppositions which we need to seek out, bring to the conscious level, and proceed to analyze and judge (*krinein*) whether they are valid or not. This is an endless task, for all the information we gather is accepted into *our* cognitive faculties, that is, they are necessarily poured into our mental containers, our *pre*suppositions, or, in a term frequently used today, into our *paradigms*. A typical example of a *paradigm* is: earlier all astronomical data was poured into the paradigm (*pre*supposition) that the Earth was the center of the planetary system, rather than the later paradigm that the Sun was the center.

But how do we find our *un* conscious *pre*-suppositions so that we may analyze and judge them? There is no sure way other than endless reflection and self-examination. However, one major help is to enter into *ongoing* Dialogues, for when sufficient mutual trust is built, our Dialogue partners will then be able to point out some of our *un*conscious *pre*suppositions, which they can see but we cannot. Our trusted Dialogue partners, thus, become for us mirrors in which we can see how at least a part of the world perceives us.

d. Intuitive Thinking

The pattern of thinking just laid out is usually called *discursive* thinking, coming from the Latin *cursus*, "run" – from whence our term "course," a path we *run* through, comes. In everyday life, however, once we have "run" a "course" of thought/activity sufficiently often, we tend to shorten the thought process so that it even becomes instantaneous. We don't have to "run" the "course" A is E, E is C… and so forth. Rather, we are able to "short circuit" (shorten the *cursus*) the process and *im*-mediately see that A is E. This thought pattern is called "intuition," from the Latin *intueri* (*in* + *tueri*, to look at, contemplate). Hence, often our thought processes are less discursive and more intuitive. This makes life much more fluid and we're able to accomplish things otherwise impossible—things otherwise "unthinkable"! How could we ever play a Chopin prelude if we always had to think c, d, f, c, c….?

21

No, having *run* through the *course* of c, f, c, c….
innumerable times, we no longer discursively think of the
link between c, d…. we *im*mediately, *intuitively* make the
linkage.

Such "intuitive" thinking and consequent action is clearly
a great boon to human living. In fact, we strive to move
our thinking/action from the discursive to the intuitive as
much as possible. This is what we do in order to develop
"virtues" – which are habitual, automatic ways of acting
positively, e.g., courageously, honestly, prudently…. We
"unthinkingly" react courageously, that is, we do not
discursively, but rather, *intuitively* think/act courageously.

As wonderful, indeed, even essential, as intuitive
thinking/acting is, to that same extent we must also subject
it to the identical kind of deep reflection as our discursive
reasoning, asking the three "W" questions of What,
Whence, Whither? Even more so with our routine,
intuitive thinking do we have to work at raising our
unconscious presuppositions to the conscious level so we
can probe, test, and analyze them to ferret out any errors
imbedded in them. This will be all the more challenging
because most often we are unaware that we are intuitively
thinking/acting in certain ways. We are often unconscious
that we are operating with innumerable "intuitions." How
often, for example, do we encournter someone for the first
time and quickly form an impression: (s)he is open,
narrow-minded, orderly? Perhaps it was the way the
person was dressed, spoke, posture, made eye contact….
none of which we consciously thought about, but
unconsciously observed and consequently made a
judgment (*krinein*!) about the person. In short, our finely

developed intuitions are wonderful. But even more wonderful is our being *conscious* of their work!

5. Emotional Intelligence/Imagination

Since the latter decades of the 20th century,[5] increased attention is being paid to what is often referred to as "Emotional Intelligence." This is an important, but not crystal clear, field of investigation. Our emotions can lead us to do many wonderful, and not so wonderful, things. We often claim that we want to free our actions from the sway of our emotions and place them under the guidance of our clear-thinking intellect. In general, such a goal appears desirable, but that is not the focus of the investigation of our "Emotional Intelligence."

Rather, the focus of Emotional Intelligence is learning how we humans can effectively mature "emotionally." Basically, that means learning to know and understand: 1) oneself, 2) other persons, and 3) how appropriately to relate to each other (this dimension leads some scholars/practitioners also at times to speak of *social* intelligence – for the sake of simplicity, I include the social dimension within the term "emotional intelligence"). One may have learned to analyze a situation with impeccable syllogistic logic (*Critical Thinking*), but be totally blind about how you yourself, or/and others, fit into the puzzle. An example of such an extreme disjunction might be that

---

[5] See Daniel Goleman, *Emotional Intelligence* (1995).

of a brilliant Critical Thinker in the body of socially oblivious person, a so-called *Idiot Savant*.

Here, too, is where the older term "Imagination" fits. In many ways "Imagination" seeks to name what the recently more popular term "Paradigm" is also – but in a more limited, "ideational," way – to after. The way we "Imagine" the world, or a particular portion of it, massively affects how we think about the world, or that portion of it, and hence, how we act in it. It is the Imagination that is the main source of human creativity. It is what makes a human "like God," an "*Imago Dei*," "Image of God." For example, if you imagine the world flat, you will act in one set of ways, but if you imagine it as a globe, you will act in another set of ways – like being the first human (Magellan) in 200,000 years – that is, *ever* – to sail around it!

The most recent research into *Emotional Intelligence/Imagination* suggests that the brain, rather than operating in separate layers of evolutionarily developed parts (e.g., "lizard brain," etc.), in fact operates cooperatively as a whole, keeping us alive and operating effectively. It does this by sifting through all the incoming sense data, comparing it with past data and an analysis of it, then making a judgment, a "prediction," that "this" is what is going on, and the proper response is "that"[6] –

---

[6] Lisa Feldman Barrett, "Emotional Intelligence Needs a Rewrite, Nautilus, http://nautil.us/issue/51/limits/emotional-intelligence-needs-a-rewrite, retrieved August 28, 2017.

amazingly, much like Thomas Aquinas in the 13th century and Aristotle before him in the 4th century BCE maintained!

Professor Lisa Feldman Barrett describes the scene this way: "This constant storm of predictions – which occur automatically and completely outside of your awareness – forms the basis for everything you think, feel, see, smell, or otherwise experience in any way. That's how emotions, thoughts, and perceptions are made." She then brings in the concept of emotional *granularity,*[7] - noting that "my students and I discovered it about 20 years ago."

This is a critical point to attend to, namely, how important it is to *learn new words* in order to actually experience different levels of experience! She notes, "when you learn new words, you sculpt your brain's microwiring, giving it the means to construct new emotional experiences…. People who exhibit high emotional granularity are emotion experts. Their brains can automatically construct emotional experiences with fine differences…. How do you enable your brain to create a wider variety of emotions and improve your emotional intelligence? One approach is to learn new emotion words. Each new word seeds your brain with the capacity to make new emotion predictions, which your brain can employ as a tool to

---

[7] The term "granularity" suggests that the thought has been separated into many very tiny individual grains so that tiny, but important, differences can be discerned.

construct your future experiences and perceptions, and to direct your actions."

The goal of maturing our Emotional-Intelligence/Imagination is not something completely new under the sun, however. St. Augustine of Hippo pointed to it when in the 5th century he uttered the prayer, asking: "To know you O God, and myself!" Clearly our Emotional-Intelligence/Imagination needs to be expanded in tandem with our Critical Thinking, and then expressed in Competitive-Cooperation action – all of which clearly takes place within the all-encompassing embrace of Deep Dialogue.

6. Closing the Loop: Competitive-Cooperation

If our *actions* are to be compatible with *Deep-Dialogue/Critical-Thinking/Emotional-Intelligence/Imagination*, they must strive toward being *Competitive-Cooperative*. Let me explain this last seemingly contradictory dual term.

If the way we understand the world determines the way we act in the world, then action completes the circle of *perception-thought-imagine-decision-act*! We first perceive, then try to understand/imagine, in light of which we make a decision, and finally act, putting our perceptions, understanding, and decisions into concrete behavioral form. If we engage the world in a deeply dialogical manner and critically analyzed-synthesized-imagined our perceptions and thoughts, we will want to make decisions on that basis, and carry out our actions in the world in an analogously Dialogic-Critical-Emotionally-Intelligent-Imagined manner. I am suggesting that the most appropriate way to describe such action is "Competitive-Cooperation."

The outcome of our *Deep-Dialogue* and *Critical-Thinking/Emotional-Intelligence/Imagination* must be our free/responsible action because the core of being human is freedom/and its corresponding responsibility. This freedom/responsibility core has always been the case since the emergence of *homo sapiens sapiens* 200,000 years ago in central Africa, even though this core freedom/

responsibility did not begin to be *de facto* widespread and recognized until around two hundred years ago with the Enlightenment. Our core human freedom/responsibility flows from our humanly developed rational intellect which allows us to "abstract" (Latin: *ab*, "from" and *tractus*, "pulled," as in "tractor") from our myriad sense perceptions various concepts and possibilities, on the basis of which we can choose, decide to act one way or another. This is another way to say we "love," i.e., we reach out to become one with what we perceive to be the "good" – for example, becoming one with the "good" ice cream, the "good" Mozart music, the "good" friend each in its appropriate way.

Humans have long recognized that we are unique in the cosmos (there may be other free beings we have not yet discovered) because of our radical freedom (despite its limitations, of which we are increasingly becoming aware) based on our rationality.

I have written extensively – and am very deliberately restressing here! – about how humanity has in the last two centuries increasingly come to realize that because all knowledge is necessarily limited, it is interpreted by the knower – "*Nobody* knows *Everything* about *Anything* – therefore *Dialogue!*"[8] Hence, we have no other intelligent

---

[8] See, e.g., Leonard Swidler, "Nobody Knows Everything about Anything! The Cosmic Dance of Dialogue," *Journal of Ecumenical Studies*, 45, 2 (Spring, 2010), 175-177, and Reflections at the Scottish Parliament at youtube.com/watch?v=Nu4ssQHRLP0.

choice but to reach out in Dialogue, *Deep Dialogue*, to those who think differently from us to learn increasingly, endlessly more about reality. I have also increasingly stressed the other side of our "coin of humanity," *Critical Thinking*, wherein we constantly pose the critical *Three "W" Questions*: *What* precisely are we talking about? *Whence* comes the basis for affirming it? *Whither* do its implications lead – *reductio ad absurdum*, or not? Steven Pinker has most recently brilliantly shown that it is the increasing human rationality, in the sense of the increasing development of reasonable habits of mind, abstract thinking, and thence actions, that is leading to an increasingly peaceful human world (counterintuitive though that may at first blush seem).[9] Even before him, in a more philosophical than social scientific manner, Bernard Lonergan also argued that increasing intelligence was a necessity for an increasingly ethical behavior.[10]

Since we humans are also bodies, our perceptions, reflections, and decisions need to result in actions in the world. Through fostering our Critical-Thinking, Emotional-Intelligence, Imagination and reaching out to increasingly expand our necessarily myopic view of

---

.

[9] Steven Pinker, *The Better Angels of Our Nature. Why Violence Has Declined* (New York: Viking Books, 2011), Chapter 9. Amazingly, it is a proven fact that the popular IQ level has steadily gone up in the U.S. over the past century in the area of abstract thinking.

[10] See Bernard Lonergan, *Method in Theology* (New York: Herder and Herder, 1972), 253. More details in Swidler, *After the Absolute* (Minneapolis: Fortress Press, 1990).

reality through *Deep-Dialogue*, we will want to act in a manner which is a reflection of our "both-and" Deep-Dialogue, Critical-Thinking, Emotional-Intelligence, Imagination namely, by Competitive-Cooperation. The "Cooperation" half of this term is relatively easy to understand. So long as the Other is not acting in a destructive manner, then we would want to act, at a minimum, not negatively toward the Other, but as much as possible in tandem, so as to create a win-win situation as much as possible.

But "Competitive"? That would seem necessarily to aim at a win-lose, zero-sum approach. To a certain extent that is accurate. However, I mean first "Competition" as with ourself, striving to be as effective, efficient, and creative as possible. If I may borrow from Islam the first meaning of *Jihad*, the Great *Jihad*: (Arabic: "struggle") – the Competition is first with ourself to live out our inner principles, placed there by God, according to Islam (and Judaism and Christianity as well). This *Creative* Competition may at times mean that one individual, one group, will get the contract, will be chosen to provide the requested product or service – win-lose, zero-sum in that sense. But the *Creative* Competitive individual and group should thereby be led to create, develop, new alternatives – as, for example, renewable energy sources as alternatives to fossil fuels, or President Obama inviting Hillary Clinton into his cabinet. In the business field, an ever more human organization increasingly searches for the most creative, expansive, all-inclusive way of operating – a "both-and," a "win-win" for both the producers and users, reflecting the creative balance of *Deep-Dialogue*, "pro-and-con," *Critical-Thinking,*

Emotional-Intelligence, Imagination in a balance of Creative Competition and Cooperation.

A striking example of such thinking – and action – in the global corporate world was given by Ryuzaburo Kaku, Chairman of the Board of the Japanese multinational Canon, Inc. His vision in leading his company convinced me that what I in English terms describe as *Competitive-Cooperation* was in fact doable. He expressed his vision as the *Kyosei* principles: "Living and working together for the common good." He argued that this concept of *Kyosei* should be a creed that all corporations and nations follow, and outlined the progress of ethical companies through four stages, describing the fourth stage thus:

The fourth type is the "corporation assuming global social responsibilities," a "truly global corporation." This type of company cares for all its direct stakeholders, including its local community – but it goes beyond: it strives to fulfill its corporate obligations on a global scale. Its social responsibilities transcend national boundaries.

Mr. Kaku was not a naive do-gooder, but a creative business entrepreneur, insisting that constant innovation was the key to creating ever more wealth for humanity – and his company: "By creating new products and pro-cesses...the company will not only succeed financially, but will also have made the world a better place to live. That is what it means to be an ethical business leader!" He also wrote: "Competition is vital for efficiency, but it must be 'fair' competition, based on innovation, quality, and effi-ciency," combining thereby "competition" with "coopera-tion": "Innovative corporations with specialties in differ-ent areas can also work together in the spirit of *Kyosei* to produce outstanding products. In this way a synergy is created and products can be produced that neither company alone could develop."

Impressive as this vision is, Kaku *Sensei* (a Japanese term for a revered teacher) later projected a stunningly challenging fifth stage:

I have recently come to believe that a fifth category is needed in my analysis of companies as they evolve into ethical social institutions. This fifth type I see as a company that *[1]* seeks to change the world for the better. Companies in the fifth stage also *[2]* try to increase the number of like-minded partners that assume global social responsibilities and that are actively concerned with global problems.... Companies in the fifth stage *[3]* realize it is not right for the enormous number of corporations existing in the world to remain apathetic about the various perplexing problems emerging on our planet. They know *[4]* it is it not enough for a corporation to transform itself only into a fourth type of corporation and simply strive to correct imbalances – it knows *[5]* it must go further.

Kaku *Sensei* would have *Kyosei* serve as a key principle in the new world order emerging after the end of the Cold War. He insisted that democracy, human rights, and peace are indeed indispensable values, but alone they are not adequate. Said another way: they are necessary, but not sufficient, causes of the common weal; *Kyosei* needs to augment them. In English terms for *Kyosei*, I offer *Competitive-Cooperation.*

In summary, the Competitive-Cooperation person/group in putting into action in a manner in keeping with Deep-

Dialogue, Critical-Thinking, Emotional-Intelligence, Imagination:

1. Is not satisfied with the passable, but reaches for the best;

2. Strives to make decisions within broader frameworks;

3. Is not satisfied with the standard, but stresses constant creativity;

4. As much as possible, avoids zero-sum, win-lose solutions, but seeks creatively win-win ones;

5. Prefers not either-or, but both-and choices.

7. "Spiritual"-Aikido

Clearly *mens sana in corpore sano* (a healthy mind in a healthy body) is a truism which needs to be taken utterly seriously. Moreover, one does not accomplish the goal of living a Deep-Dialogue Whole-Human life simply by exercising the body *alongside* the mind. A human is an *integrated* body-spirit. Hence, if not Aikido, then certainly something like it which integrates the body and soul and also facilitates the positive encounter with the Other is needed.

What is so suitable about Aikido is its strong stress on the interior, integrating the spiritual dimension with physical exercise and training. Hence, a *Deep-Dialogue Whole-Human* life needs Aikido, or its equivalent, thereby providing a "closing of the circle" of the Whole-Human sequence: "*Encounter – Reflection – Motivation – Decision – Action*," that is: 1) Deep Dialogue, 2) Critical Thinking, 3) Emotional Intelligence/Imagination, 4) Competitive Cooperation, 5) "Spiritual"-Aikido.

Aikido is a Japanese martial art which was developed by Morihei Ueshiba over an extended period, 1927 to his death in 1969. Again, the point is not to choose one martial art over others, or to choose a martial art at all. Rather, Aikido makes sense in structuring a *Deep-Dialogue Whole-Human* life because, as its name reflects (合 – *ai* – Unifying, 気 – *ki* – Energy, 道 – *dō* – Way), that is, "The Way of Unifying Energy," pulls together the "Whole Human Being," body and spirit, including her/his relationship to the Other – even at the extreme when the Other is hostile – in a fashion which integrates the Other in a positive, "cooperative" way. The essence of Aikido is to learn to unite the whole of one's being, interiorly and exteriorly, and then use the energy and thrust of an attacking Other to disarm him non-violently, thereby turning him, if not into a dialogue partner, at least a nondestructive Other – a first step toward Dialogue.

8. Golden Rule

a. Background

The *Golden Rule* – "Love your neighbor as yourself" – is doubtless the most widely known and affirmed ethical principle worldwide. At the same time, it has its serious, quasi-serious, and jocund critics. There are also variations of the Golden Rule, i.e., the so-called *Silver Rule* (the negative articulation: "You should not do to your neighbor what you do not want done to yourself"), as well as the extrapolated *Platinum Rule* version:[11] "You should treat your neighbor as s/he wishes to be treated." It is worthwhile to spend some energy on each of these variations and critics, but then most of all I would like to reflect on the meaning, implications, and applications of the *Golden Rule* for the 21st century.

Let me deal with the jocund first to get it out of the way:

Question: What does the sadist say to the masochist when the latter says: *Beat me!*?

Answer: *No!*

---

[11] Perhaps first articulated by Karl Popper, *The Open Society and Its Enemies*, vol. 2 (1966 [1945]), 386.

This (per)version of the Golden Rule might be good for a party joke, but it – and its variations, including some of its allegedly "serious" critiques – are good for nothing more.

b. Early Versions of the Golden Rule

Perhaps, the earliest recorded "predecessor" to the Golden Rule was expressed in ancient Egypt in the story of "The Eloquent Peasant," recorded sometime between 2040–1650 BCE: "Do to the doer to make him do," which is a version of the later Roman principle *do ut des*, "I give so that you will give" – a principle of reciprocity, *quid pro quo*.

The earliest versions of the Golden Rule all appeared roughly at the same time, in the 6th century BCE, and all save one were really the so-called "Silver Rule," that is, negative versions of the Golden Rule. These three "Silver Rule" versions were by: Zarathustra in Persia ("Whatever is disagreeable to yourself do not do unto others." *Shayast-na-Shayast* 13:29); Confucius in China ("What you do not wish for yourself, do not do to others." *Analects* XV.24); and Thales in Greece ("Avoid doing what you would blame others for doing." None of his writings have survived; what we know of him comes from later writers). The fourth 6th century BCE articulation was truly the Golden Rule, that is, the positive version; it is recorded in the Bible ("Love your neighbor as yourself. I am Yahweh!" Lev 19:18).

It is interesting to note that these four most ancient articulations of the "Gold/Silver Rule" all appeared in the Axial Age (8th to 2nd century BCE), so named by the German philosopher Karl Jaspers.[12] He noted that in the four most ancient civilizations – Mesopotamia, Greece, the Indus River Valley, and the Yellow River Valley – there occurred a fundamental paradigm shift from human identity being experienced primarily as a member of the tribe, to as a unique person – e.g., according to Socrates: "Only the [personally] examined life is worth living!" Hence, one was to aid not only fellow tribe members who were in distress, but *all persons*.

It is also interesting to note that the Israelite/Judaic tradition of the ancient Axial Age not only is the sole ancient source which states the true (positive) version of the Golden Rule, but also articulates the negative "*Silver* Rule" version: E.g., the 3rd-century biblical book Tobit: "Do to no one what you yourself dislike" (Tobit 4:15); and the famous story about the teacher of Rabbi Yeshua ha-Notzri (that is, Rabbi Jesus of Nazareth), Rabbi Hillel, who, when asked by a Gentile whether he could summarize the whole of ethics while standing on one foot (Rabbi Shammai, Hillel's conservative "competitor" was previously asked the same thing, but boxed the Gentile's ears and sent him away), said: "What is hateful to you, do not do to your fellow: this is the whole Torah; the rest is explanation; go and learn." (Btal. Shabbath folio:31a)

---

[12] Karl Jaspers, Vom Ursprung und Ziel der Geschichte, 1949 (The Origin and Goal of History, 1953).

However, as noted above, already centuries earlier the positive version, the true *Golden* Rule, was first articulated – at the same time as Zarathustra's, Confucius' and Thalis' negative, *Silver* versions – in the 6th century BCE. It is found in the Bible: "You shall love your neighbor as yourself" (Lev 19:34). Subsequently, in the early part of the first century CE, this passage was quoted by Rabbi Yeshua in this positive Golden Rule, form (Mt 7:12). It is interesting to note that Yeshua's exact contemporary (at least regarding their presumed birth dates), the Roman Stoic, Seneca the Younger (4 BCE–65 CE) also articulated the positive Golden Rule in his essay regarding the treatment of slaves: "Treat your inferior as you would wish your superior to treat you." (Seneca, *41. Slaves*)

c. The Platinum Rule

Let's look next at the "newcomer, the so-called "Platinum Rule": "You should treat your neighbor as *s/he* wishes to be treated." This attempt at improving the Golden Rule argues along this line: I, as a meat-eater, should not feed my hungry vegetarian neighbor "as myself" (i.e., with meat), but as "(s)he would want." However, that principle would then also dictate that the good neighbor should give the drug addict more drugs when (s)he is "in need," an undesired absurdity. Such a "Platinum Rule" proposed as an "improvement" or "correction" of the Golden Rule appears to deliberately misconstrue and empty the clear meaning of the positive Golden Rule.

Of course, the acting person, the "agent," in the food example above, would (s)he, her/himself want to receive nourishing, pleasing food were (s)he hungry, and therefore (s)he should treat the hungry neighbor similarly were (s)he hungry. If the "recipient" were, for example, a hungry President H.W. Bush (who notoriously hated broccoli), the "agent" would realize that the Golden Rule meant that (s)he should give H.W. Bush nourishing food other than broccoli. It is clear that the meaning of the Golden Rule – in regard to food, as an example – is that just as the "agent" would want nourishing, pleasing food were (s)he hungry, s/he should provide the same nourishing, pleasing food, which, were the recipient a vegetarian, would not include meat. Hence, the so-called "Platinum Rule," rather than being a correction or improvement of the Golden Rule, is an unhelpful distortion of it.

d. *Rabbi Yeshua (Jesus) and the Golden Rule*

Let's take a further look at the "full" Golden Rule, the positive articulation. It takes on a hugely expanded role in Christianity, for it turns up in multiple articulations in the Bible, and subsequently in Jewish Rabbinical writings and in Yeshua's teaching and later Christian writers. It is interesting that unlike his teacher Rabbi Hillel – whose famous encounter with the Gentile evinced a negative "Silver Rule" version – Rabbi Yeshua's articulation was of the positive Golden Rule version. We have it recorded twice, once in Matthew's Gospel and once in Luke's. That means that both Matthew and Luke found this maxim in their common source, which today scholars refer to as *Q*

Sayings of Jesus.[13] In Matthew, Yeshua says, "Treat others as you would have them treat you; that is the meaning of the Law and the Prophets" (Mt 7:12), Luke records Yeshua saying: "Treat others as you as would have them treat you" (Lk 6:31). Let's add to the mix the remark of Paul of Tarsus in his letter to the Romans as he was under house arrest in Rome awaiting trial – and, as it turned out, eventual execution. He wrote: "Owe no one anything except to love one another, for whoever loves the other fulfills the law (Rm 13:8).

Both Matthew's and Paul's articulations end saying that keeping the Golden Rule fulfills the "Law," *Nomos* (which is the Jewish Septuagint Greek translation of the Hebrew *Torah* – more accurately translated in English as "teaching"; but over the centuries the "teachings" hardened in its understanding to mean "law"). Something similar happened to the Hebrew term *ha lacha* ("the way"), which also hardened to mean "law" (*halacha*), and similarly its later Semitic neighbor Islamic Arabic *Shariah* (the "way") hardened in Islam to mean the "law." However, Luke's version mentions nothing about "the law," *Nomos*.

13

See http://web.archive.org/web/19990219224131/http://www.augustana.ab.ca/~bjor s/q-english.htm, *The Critical Text of Q,* 1996, International Q Project. This is the English translation of the text of Q as it has been reconstructed by the International Q Project of the Society of Biblical Literature, as of November 1996.

The question asks itself: Why did Matthew and Paul include the reference to *Nomos* (*Torah*) and Luke not? The different backgrounds and addressees of the different Gospel writers yield the answer: Matthew is clearly – judging from his Hebrew-tinted Greek language, and his constant saying that "such and such was done to fulfill the (Hebrew) prophet X, who said…." – a very knowledgeable Jew who is writing for fellow Jews. Paul was a learned Hellenist Jew who was also intensely Jewish, describing himself as a "Pharisee of Pharisees." He was writing mainly to fellow Greek-speaking Hellenist Jews. On the other hand, Luke was a Greek-speaking follower of Paul and was writing for Greek speakers, who did not know much Hebrew and Jewish history or scripture. Fulfilling the *Torah*, *Nomos*, would have had little significance for them, whereas eternal life would.

e. The Greatest Commandment

The Golden Rule comes up again in another section of the Gospels, this time in response to a question put to Yeshua about the "Greatest Commandment," and it appears in all three of the synoptic Gospels. The oldest of the three is Mark's, where a scribe asks Rabbi Yeshua what the first (*prote*) commandment is, and Yeshua responds with a lengthy quotation from the Torah about loving God totally, and then continues: "And the second is this: You shall love your neighbor as you love yourself. There is no commandment greater than these." (Mk 12: 28-34)

Matthew's report is similar, except that it is a Pharisaic lawyer, not a scribe, who asks the question: "What is the great commandment in the Law (*Nomos*)?" Yeshua answered that the first commandment is the love of God, and "the second is similar, you shall love your neighbor as yourself. On these two, hang all the Law (*Nomos*) and the prophets." (Mt 22:34-40 – Note, summarizing the 603 biblical laws in these two "Greatest Laws" was also done, as we saw above, by Yeshua's teacher Rabbi Hillel.)

f. Rabbi Yeshua Was Not a Christian – He Was a Jew

Parenthetically, it is important to note that by linking these two commandments together in Matthew's Gospel, Rabbi Yeshua did not ignore the Jewish tradition, but in fact very much adhered to it! Perhaps two hundred years before Yeshua was born, other Jewish writers stated much the same "combining" sentiments. They are found in various passages of the Pseudepigrapha (noncanonical Jewish writings in Greek): "Love the Lord and the neighbor" (*Testament of Issachar* 5:2); "I loved the Lord and every human being with my whole heart" (ibid., 7:6); "Love the Lord in your whole life and one another with a sincere heart" (*Testament of Daniel* 5:3); "Fear the Lord and love the neighbor" (*Testament of Benjamin* 3:3); "And he commanded them to keep to the way of God, do justice, and everyone love his/her neighbor" (*Jubilees* 20:9); "Love one another my sons as brothers, as one loves oneself .... You should love one another as yourselves" (ibid., 36:4-6). Precisely the same summing up of the Law, *Torah*, in the double commandment of love was expressed by a slightly older Jewish contemporary of Yeshua, Philo of Alexandria c. 20 BCE-50 CE). In the tractate, "Concerning Individual Commandments," II, 63, he wrote: "There are, so to speak, two fundamental teachings to which the numberless individual teachings and statements

46

are subordinated: in reference to God the commandment of honoring God and piety, in reference to humanity that of the love of humanity (*phil-anthropia*) and justice."

g. *Rabbi Yeshua, Like a Peripatetic Greek Philosopher*

Luke's version is essentially the same – first commandment, "love of God," second commandment, "love of neighbor" – but with some intriguing variations. First, the lawyer (*Nomikos*) asked Rabbi Yeshua, not what the greatest commandment is, but "'Rabbi, what should I do to inherit eternal life?' And he said to him, 'What is written in the Law (*Nomos*)? How do you read?' He responded, 'You should love God with your whole heart…. and your neighbor as yourself.' And he said to him, 'You have answered correctly. Do this and you will live'" (Lk 10:25-28). Second, it is not Yeshua who cites Torah about the two greatest commandments, but the lawyer!

As noted above, the lawyer does not ask what the greatest commandment is, but "what must I do to gain eternal life?" Clearly, such a concern would be more existential to Hellenist Greek readers than the carrying out of some ancient law. Even more amazing, the answer is not given by Rabbi Yeshua, but, through a typically Greek "Socratic dialogue" Yeshua asks the lawyer to answer his own question. Here the Greek Luke does not present "a rabbi teaching the Hebrew Torah," but on a "Hellenized peripatetic[14] 'Socratic' teacher." (Note, "Teacher" is what "Rabbi" means. The Gospels in general translate "Rabbi" Yeshua as *Didaskalos* – Greek, "teacher"). It would seem that the Hellenist Luke is appealing here to his culturally Greek readership, portraying his hero, Jesus, acting like a good teacher, *Didaskalos*, stimulating his student to think. Also, as noted, Luke's lawyer, *Nomikos*, does not ask what the "Greatest Commandment" is – which would be important for Jews, but not for Hellenists. Nevertheless, Hellenists would be very interested in "Eternal Life!"

Luke's Gospel here is also special. After Yeshua said to the *Nomikos,* "You have answered correctly. Do this and you shall live," it says that the *Nomikos*, "wishing to justify himself, said…." "Justify himself?" How so? The answer lies in Matthew's rendition of the beginning of the scene, where it notes that the *Nomikos*, "tempting him, asks…." (Mt 22: 35), tried to catch Rabbi Yeshua in a debater's ploy, but when Yeshua turned the tables and asked him to answer his own question, he clearly felt chagrined, and "wishing to justify himself, he asked Jesus, 'Who is my neighbor?'" (Lk 10: 29) Yeshua, like a good rabbi, answered the question with a question by way of a story – the well-known narrative of the "Good Samaritan."

To recall the kernel of the story, a Jew was robbed, beaten, and left at the roadside; then a priest walked past him,

---

[14] Greek, "walking/conversing," as was said of Aristotle's *Lyceum* students with professor.

followed by a Levite (both high-level Jews, of course), and then a Samaritan (hated with a passion by Jews) stopped and cared for him, brought him to an inn and paid for his convalescence. Rabbi Yeshua again, like a good Greek Socratic teacher, made the *Nomikos* once more answer his own question: Who is my neighbor? His answer: The (hated!) Samaritan.

Elsewhere (Mt 25:31-45), Yeshua made it clear that for him "the neighbor" meant especially those who were in need: You should give drink to the thirsty, food to the hungry, clothe the naked, visit the sick, visit those in prison; God says, Whatever you have done to these most despised, you have done to me!

It is important, especially for Westerners, and most especially Christians, to note that Yeshua was not a Christian, but a Jew, even a rabbi! He did not, as many Christians believed for many centuries, reject the Law and Judaism; he was not a Christian antinomian ("against the *Nomos*, Law"): "Do not think that I came to abolish the Law or the prophets; I came not to abolish, but to carry out" (*plerosai*, literally, to *implement*; Mt 5:17-19).

h. Rabbi Yeshua and Others Push Beyond the "Requirements"

However, even then, Rabbi Yeshua insisted that the whole of the Torah should be carried out not according to the letter, but according to its spirit. He went beyond it, holding out the ideal of a "self-emptying" (*kenosen*, as Paul said in Greek in Phil 2:7) love. For Yeshua, it was not a question of living *either* by the letter of the Law, the Torah, *or* its spirit, but rather, living the *whole* Law

49

(Torah) according to its *spirit*: Not freedom *from* the Law, but freedom *through* the Law, *and beyond* to a self-emptying kenotic love (*kenosen*, as Paul said in Greek in Phil 2:7), love for one's friends, one's neighbors, even one's enemies – as seen especially in the Sermon on the Mount (Mt 5ff.). The ancient rabbis had a phrase for these halachic (religious laws) decisions which went beyond the demands of the Torah: *Lifnim meshurat hadin* ("beyond the requirements of the court"):

Proto-rabbis [Rabbi Philip Sigal's term for Yeshua and other Jewish religious leaders like Hillel, Shammai, and others] sometimes encouraged going beyond the strict requirement of law or the literal reading of a text. In this way they inspired some to sacrifice their monetary or property right under law in order to extend equity to others. This is how we are to understand Mt 5:40 ["And if anyone sue you at law and take away your coat, let him have your cloak as well."].[15]

Four hundred years later the Christian follower of Rabbi Yeshua, St. Augustine of Hippo, expressed the same thought in different words: *Ama, et fac quod vis*, "Love, and do what you will," for your love will lead you not contrary to the Law, but to it, and beyond.

However, what was most special about Yeshua was that he *lived* not only according to the Torah, but also according to his supererogatory kenotic ideal, *lifnim meshurat*

---

[15] Philip Segal, *The Halakhah of Jesus according to the Gospel of Matthew*, (Society of Biblical Literature: 2007), 79.

hadin – even to the point of dying for the sake of his friends: "Greater love than this has no one, but that he gives his life for his friends" [that is, for "those loved by him," *ton philon autou*, Jn 15:13].

Both the later Jewish, and then Muslim traditions expanded even that totally altruistic stance: In the sayings of Rabbi Nathan we find: "To whomever saves a single soul [Self] it is reckoned as if (s)he saved the whole world .... To whomever destroys a single soul [Self] it is reckoned as if s/he destroyed the whole world .... From this you learn that one human is worth the whole of creation" (*Mishnah*: Aboth Rabbi Nathan 31).[16]

At the same time, one also finds in the Qur'an: "Whoever kills an innocent human being, it shall be as if he has killed all humankind, and whoever saves the life of one, it shall be as if he had saved the life of all humankind" (*Qur'an*: 5:32). The near identity in these two religion's "revelations" is amazing. According to them, it is God's teaching according to the Torah and the Qur'an that the individual human Person/Self is worth, and worthy of, the whole of creation.

A follower of Rabbi Yeshua took his teaching/living of a life of love a final step further to the ultimate source of the Golden Rule: *Ho theos agape estin*! God *is* love! (1 John).

---

[16] Aboth Rabbi Nathan 31, quoted in Paul Billerbeck, *Kommentar zum Neuen Testament aus Talmud und Midrasch* (Munich, 1922), I, 750.

i. Conclusion

We saw that the recent so-called *Platinum Rule,* that is, "Do to others what they would want you to do them" is a deceptive mirage. The so-called *Silver Rule,* the negative version of the *Golden Rule,* namely, "Do not do to others what you would not want them to do to yourself," was a huge human advance that was first articulated in the 6th century BCE, the center of the *Axial Age* (800-200 BCE), by Thales of Greece, Zarathustra of Persia, and Confucius of China, and in the Hebraic tradition, also in the 6th century. However, there was a profound difference between the "nicknamed" *Silver Rule* and the true, *Golden Rule,* also first articulated in the 6th century BCE in Israel.

The *Golden Rule,* as we have seen, is truly open-ended, and especially the three Abrahamic religions, Judaism, Christianity, and Islam, have continued to push that open-ended quality much farther than the *Silver Rule.* We have seen that the *Golden Rule* leads to (but does not *mandate)* the ever-expanding borders of the love of the other so that it embraces ultimately all humans, all creation, to the Beginning/End of Reality.

Hence, the *Golden Rule* leads to the opposite of restricting one's Ego/Self. Rather, it fosters the *expansion* of one's Ego/Self beyond the cage of one's skin to embrace one's neighbor, all humans, all living beings, inanimate matter, nonmaterial reality.... becoming an endlessly expanding Self/Ego. It implies open-endedly becoming one with – to as "described" by 13th-century Thomas Aquinas as – *Ipsum Esse subsistens* (Latin, *Subsisting Being Itself*) – customarily named "God," but by the deepest thinkers: *Das Nichts, Sunyata, Brahman, Dao, Process*

8. Conclusion

At a time when the Internet and our cell phones have reduced our dialogues to phrases or an emoji —and we have become a people who respond in this abbreviated way—we have lost one of the keys to communicating with each other on a deeper level. Often, we don't seem to notice the warmth that is missing. We need each other to grow and expand our thought process; to bounce ideas off one another. We need to reach outside ourselves and explore different cultures. To grow from within. Dialogue….communicating. These are extremely important to our existence.

Yes, much of our dialogue is needed to keep our everyday lives intact. But what about those moments of discussion about things we believe to be true, whether it be philosophy, religion, politics, anything of value. Maybe, because we "know" what we believe to be true, we have never considered that what we believe may not be true. Consider for a moment those holiday family gatherings. Most homes demand, no discussion of religion or politics. This is common throughout our country, because it can cause such a rift between family members that many don't speak to each other for the entire following year.

After exploring the process and roots/origins of words within these pages, we now see where all of this begins, and even more importantly, how our dialogue can go awry and this misinterpretation can lead us astray.

What if things as simple as our family gatherings could be different? What if a discussion on the world stage could be different? What if?

This is not a new way of thinking. It has been around for a while, but still some have never grasped it. It is based on truth and gives us a chance to question the validity of what we believe. It gives us the chance to discover if we have the wrong premise to begin with which may lead us to the wrong conclusion. So, the best way to do this is to be sure we start with a truth (fact), and if that has not been established, do the research and get the real answer. It will take practice, there is no doubt, but if we learn the process laid out within these pages, it will take us to a much deeper experience and result.

Think of how it would change the dynamics in our families and close contacts if we could be open to others' ideas, their cultural differences, and facts as long as they are actually facts and we can have a discussion instead of a full-blown argument. The "my way or the highway" thought doesn't move things forward. There is nothing saying one has to adopt the other's way of thinking, but to listen and to grow, to expand our vision outside of our personal bubble.

We each have our own vision of what is. And we will cling to it until there is no tomorrow, unless a new vision becomes our reality. If we took the time to practice this process, and then invite a deep discussion of what is, I believe we could change the world, one person at a time.

Don't Miss Out on Other Books in This Series.

Visit https://ipubcloud.com/ to learn about other world-renowned authors.

Check out some of the related books to this one on the website.

Movement for a Global Ethic, Walls to Bridge The Global Ethic, Letters to Will Lessons to Live By

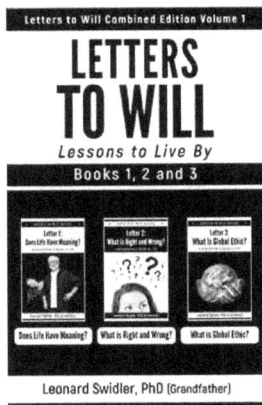

www.ingramcontent.com/pod-product-compliance
Lightning Source LLC
Chambersburg PA
CBHW072053040426
42447CB00012BB/3105